CW00429312

The Wit and Wisdom of

MARGARET THATCHER

and Other Tory Legends

Richard Benson

summersdale

THE WIT AND WISDOM OF MARGARET THATCHER

Summersdale Publishers Ltd
46 West Street
Chichester
West Sussex
PO19 1RP
UK

www.summersdale.com

Printed and bound in Great Britain

ISBN: 978-1-84953-094-1

Substantial discounts on bulk quantities of Summersdale books are available to corporations, professional associations and other organisations. For details contact Summersdale Publishers by telephone: +44 (0) 1243 771107, fax: +44 (0) 1243 786300 or email: nicky@summersdale.com.

Contents

THATCHER
ON THATCHER

I went to Oxford University – but I've never let that hold me back.

Margaret Thatcher

I was told beforehand my arrival was unscheduled, but on the way here I passed a local cinema and it turns out you were expecting me after all. The billboard read *The Mummy Returns*.

Margaret Thatcher at a Tory Election Rally in Plymouth, 22 May 2001

I hope that one quality in which
I am not lacking is courage.

Margaret Thatcher

I've got a woman's ability to stick to a
job and get on with it when everyone
else walks off and leaves it.

Margaret Thatcher

I still do the cooking myself… rush in,
peel the vegetables, put the roast in all
before I take off my hat.

Margaret Thatcher in an interview with the Telegraph, *after
becoming spokeswoman for the Treasury, March 1966*

I tend to look at things more logically
than do my colleagues.

Margaret Thatcher

I like to be made
a fuss of by a lot
of chaps.

Margaret Thatcher

I always appreciate the
other person's problem.

Margaret Thatcher

I cannot change my style. There are
many people who are reasonably
pleased that one gives a firm lead.

*Margaret Thatcher on being criticised for not always
listening and being domineering in style*

I usually make up my mind about a
man in ten seconds; and I very rarely
change it.

Margaret Thatcher

I am really very normal. I'm just a
perfectly ordinary person.

Margaret Thatcher

THE IRON
LADY SPEAKS

You turn if you want to.
The lady's not for turning.

Margaret Thatcher

If it is once again one
against 48, then I am very
sorry for the 48.

Margaret Thatcher

I don't mind how much my ministers
talk – as long as they do what I say.

Margaret Thatcher

If you lead a country like Britain...
then you have to have a touch of
iron about you.

Margaret Thatcher

Being prime minister is a lonely job...
you cannot lead from the crowd.

Margaret Thatcher

I seem to smell the stench of
appeasement in the air.

Margaret Thatcher

I am extraordinarily patient, provided I
get my own way in the end.

Margaret Thatcher

There is only one small vowel…
between ruin and run.
The small vowel… is 'I'.

Margaret Thatcher

I'm not hard, I'm frightfully soft.
But I will not be hounded.

Margaret Thatcher

I will not
change just to
court popularity.

Margaret Thatcher

I am not known for my objectives or
purposes being unclear.

Margaret Thatcher

To accuse me of being too
inflexible is poppycock.

Margaret Thatcher

I am no Darth Vader and you don't
have to protect yourselves from me.

Margaret Thatcher

OTHER TORY
LEGENDS ON
THATCHER

She was a tigress surrounded
by hamsters.

John Biffen

History will surely recognise her
achievements… a leader with the
courage of her convictions, who
assailed the conventional wisdom
of her day, challenged and overthrew
the existing order, changed the
political map, and put her country
on its feet again.

Geoffrey Howe

It is quite clear that history will record that Margaret Thatcher was the greatest prime minister this country has had since Churchill.

Nigel Lawson

The truth of the matter is that in my experience she was almost always right, and therefore there wasn't a great necessity for her to admit she was wrong.

Ian Gow

She is a formidable politician.
She has always spoken her mind.
She has a right to do it, and she will
continue to do so.

John Major

Working with a team is not
her strong point.

David Howell

I think her greatest achievement
is to have made people believe that
the impossible is possible. That the
things which were said in 1979 to be
beyond resolution, the problem of the
trade unions for example, she boldly
took it on and she did it. If politicians
can learn that lesson from her, that
there is no problem which is too big
to be solved, then she's contributed
something enormously important
to our life.

Norman Tebbit

The trouble is, we've got a corporal at
the top, not a cavalry officer.

Francis Pym

She has made a remarkable
contribution to Britain's history
and has led this country with great
distinction in the 1980s.

Michael Heseltine

I never thought of her as a woman.

John Biffen

She was like Boadicea, hammering away at those wicked people seeking to carry out policies alien to her trusted beliefs and nature.

James Prior

We were all her creation.

Kenneth Baker

Everyone likes to win arguments. She likes to win them more than most.

William Whitelaw

If Margaret Thatcher had been prime minister at the time, there would have been no Treaty of Maastricht.

Douglas Hurd

I suppose I began to like her when she made me a Cabinet Minister.

Kenneth Baker

I think it was much more a peasants'
uprising than a religious war. It was
seen much more as the overthrow of
the tyrant king rather than a great
ideological shift.

*Chris Patten on Margaret Thatcher's election to
the Tory leadership*

I tell you something she's not
very good at; she's not very good
at relaxing, taking time off. That's
the nature of the creature.
God bless her, I think.

Keith Joseph

I've always had a great respect and
been very candid with her, and I hope
the reverse is the case.

Chris Patten

She'll be prime minister until the
middle of the next century.

Jeffrey Archer

It wasn't an election.
It was an assumption.

*Norman St John-Stevas on Margaret Thatcher's election as
leader of the Conservative Party*

THE STRONGER SEX

If you want something said, ask
a man... if you want something
done, ask a woman.

Margaret Thatcher

You chaps don't like short answers.
Or direct answers. Men like long
rambly, waffly answers.

Margaret Thatcher

On what she learned during her
time in politics:
Men are not a reasoned
or reasonable sex.

Margaret Thatcher

The cocks may crow, but it's the hen
that lays the egg.

Margaret Thatcher

I owe nothing
to Women's Lib.

Margaret Thatcher

Any woman who understands the problems of running a home will be nearer to understanding the problems of running a country.

Margaret Thatcher

Most women defend themselves. It is the female of the species... which tends to defend when attacked.

Margaret Thatcher

The woman's mission is not to
enhance the masculine spirit, but
to express the feminine.

Margaret Thatcher

I don't notice that I'm a woman.
I regard myself as Prime Minister.

Margaret Thatcher

Being powerful is like being a lady.
If you have to tell people you are,
you aren't.

Margaret Thatcher

No, they seem to like ladies.

Margaret Thatcher, when asked if she was surprised that the male-dominated Conservative Party had elected her as their leader

It's easier for a woman than a man to give up his power because you are not so lost. A woman can fill the time spring-cleaning the house.

Margaret Thatcher

I'd like to get on with the job without being in the limelight all the time.

Margaret Thatcher on why she wished there were more women in parliament

KEEPING UP
APPEARANCES

I'm going to have furniture I like…
because I intend to be there a
long, long time.

Margaret Thatcher on living at Number Ten

Jim Prior: I read in my paper you had
developed a sexy voice.
Margaret Thatcher: Jim, what makes
you think I wasn't sexy before?

I adore red, but of course I can only wear it at home or on holiday. People really do comment, you know.

Margaret Thatcher

I'm here in my red chiffon evening gown... The Iron Lady of the Western world? Me?

Margaret Thatcher

You know how it is, if your hair looks awful you feel awful.

Margaret Thatcher

My hats seem
to incense
some people.

Margaret Thatcher

Now I am very sad and sorry that I
didn't make picture of the year. I think
I could have done one with the caption
on it: 'It's in the bag'.

*Margaret Thatcher on being photographed on the night of
her election*

It is expensive to be in politics...
one has to be well groomed, and
one has to entertain.

Margaret Thatcher

WHERE THERE'S
A WILLIE, THERE'S
A WAY

It is never wise to appear to be more clever than you are. It is sometimes wise to appear slightly less so.

William Whitelaw

I was one of those people who was always rather frightened of women politicians.

William Whitelaw

I have kissed her often before (but not) on a pavement outside a hotel in Eastbourne. We have done it in various rooms in one way or another at various functions. It is perfectly genuine and normal – and normal and right – to do so.

William Whitelaw, when questioned on kissing Margaret Thatcher outside the National Young Conservatives' Conference in Eastbourne

Lawless schools produce
lawless children.

William Whitelaw

I have the thermometer in my mouth
and I am listening to it all the time.

*William Whitelaw on party morale in the election campaign
of October 1974*

The Labour Party is going about the
country stirring up apathy.

William Whitelaw

THERE'S NO SUBSTITUTE FOR HARD WORK

You may have to fight a battle more
than once to win it.

Margaret Thatcher

Look at a day when you are supremely
satisfied at the end. It's not a day when
you lounge around doing nothing; it's
when you had everything to do, and
you've done it.

Margaret Thatcher

I wasn't lucky.
I deserved it.

Margaret Thatcher

I do not know anyone who has gotten
to the top without hard work. That is
the recipe. It will not always get you to
the top, but it will get you pretty near.

Margaret Thatcher

There must be no hankering
after soft options.

Margaret Thatcher

One only gets to the top rung of
the ladder by steadily climbing up
one at a time.

Margaret Thatcher

Freedom is not synonymous
with an easy life.

Margaret Thatcher

I am always on the job.

Margaret Thatcher

One thing aggravates me more than anything else – inefficiency. I can be very sharp about that.

Margaret Thatcher

Plan your work for today and every day, then work your plan.

Margaret Thatcher

We hanker after a West German
standard of output.

Margaret Thatcher

There is nothing inevitable about rising
unemployment.

Margaret Thatcher

Whatever we want to achieve, we have
to do something about it ourselves.

Margaret Thatcher

I couldn't live without work.
That's what makes me so sympathetic
towards those people who are
unemployed. I don't know how
they live without working.

Margaret Thatcher

The world has never offered
us an easy living.

Margaret Thatcher

Jobs grow not out of windy promises
and implausible targets. They spring
from individual effort.

Margaret Thatcher

I do not make forecasts
of unemployment.

Margaret Thatcher

THE TRUTH
ABOUT POLITICS

In politics, the unexpected happens.

Margaret Thatcher

The politician's prayer is: may my
words be ever soft and low, for I may
have to eat them.

Norman Lamont

In democracy everyone has the right to
be represented, even the jerks.

Chris Patten

The wisdom of hindsight, so useful
to historians and indeed to authors
of memoirs, is sadly denied to
practising politicians.

Margaret Thatcher

We're not saying, 'We're politicians,
trust us.' We know you don't trust us.

Michael Howard

In politics, it is
the half-hearted
who lose.

Margaret Thatcher

In politics people give you what
they think you deserve and deny
you what they think you want.

Cecil Parkinson

You don't tell deliberate lies, but
sometimes you have to be evasive.

Margaret Thatcher

I believe that in politics one should decide what is right and then decide the presentation, not the other way round.

Norman Lamont

MPs are divided into two categories – whips and former whips.

Cecil Parkinson

If you discover one thing over the years, it is that you cannot plan a political career.

Malcolm Rifkind

No one can win alone. Ever. You can only win by having a lot of people thinking and working the way you do. It's not a victory for Margaret Thatcher, it's not a victory for women. It is a victory for someone in politics.

Margaret Thatcher, when asked if she viewed her victory in winning Conservative Party leadership as a victory for herself alone or as a victory for women in Britain

It is better to be a has-been than
a never-was.

Cecil Parkinson

Politics is a life sentence. It's an
obsessive, all-demanding, utterly
fascinating, totally committing
profession – stimulating,
satisfying, stretching.

Michael Heseltine

ME, TARZAN

They say a man should be judged by
his enemies. I am very proud of mine.

Michael Heseltine

I am humble enough to recognise
that I have made mistakes, but
politically astute enough to have
forgotten what they are.

Michael Heseltine

Yes, I do talk to my trees. I did say
to one 'You'd better smarten yourself
up or you'll be gone' and the next year,
well, you've never seen such a
mass of flowers.

Michael Heseltine

If the basis of trust between the Prime
Minister and her Defence Secretary no
longer exists, there is no place for me
with honour in such a Cabinet.

Michael Heseltine's resignation statement, 9 January 1986

We must fight to regain a place in
our cities because by any standards
I understand they will be better
run if we do.

Michael Heseltine

I keep telling my Tory colleagues:
don't have any policies. A manifesto
that has policies alienates people.
In 1979 the manifesto said nothing,
which was brilliant.

Michael Heseltine

I always knew that Neil Kinnock
belonged in the economic nursery.
Now, God help us, we've got twins.

*Michael Heseltine on John Smith during the run-up
to the 1992 election*

The market has no morality.

Michael Heseltine

SINGING
THE BLUES

I believe the Conservative Party
is the last bastion between Britain
and disaster.

Margaret Thatcher

The fundamental question is, is the
Conservative Party leadable?

*Michael Heseltine, following William Hague's resignation as
leader of the Tories, 9 June 2001*

It behaves more like a tribe than a democratic institution... responding to custom rather than reason and using its own liturgy and language for the conduct of its domestic affairs.

Chris Patten on the Conservative Party, The Times, 10 October 1981

We're always short of money. We need a lot more. Do you think we should take a collection at the door?

Margaret Thatcher, when asked after winning Conservative leadership if she would be able to attract finance to the party

No great party can survive except on the basis of firm beliefs about what it wants to do. It is not enough to have reluctant support. We want people's enthusiasm as well.

Margaret Thatcher

An election victory such as ours is impossible without teamwork.

Margaret Thatcher

TAKING SIDES

Standing in the middle of the road is very dangerous; you get knocked down by the traffic from both sides.

Margaret Thatcher

There are still people in my party who believe in consensus politics. I regard them as quislings, as traitors... I mean it.

Margaret Thatcher

Nothing is more obstinate than a fashionable consensus.

Margaret Thatcher

To me, consensus seems to be the process of abandoning all beliefs, principles, values and policies. So it is something in which no one believes and to which no one objects.

Margaret Thatcher

If you have conviction people are much more likely to come out and support you.

Margaret Thatcher

It pays to know the enemy – not least because at some time you may have the opportunity to turn him into a friend.

Margaret Thatcher

You don't win by just being against things, you only win by being *for* things and making your message perfectly clear.

Margaret Thatcher during a press conference after winning Tory leadership

My job is to stop Britain going red.

Margaret Thatcher

DEFENCE OF
THE REALM

In the end it is not the weapons
which cause war but the people
who possess them.

Margaret Thatcher

Just rejoice at that news
and congratulate our forces
and the marines.

*Margaret Thatcher to press after the announcement that
British forces had captured South Georgia on 25 April 1982*

Democratic nations must try to find
ways to starve the terrorist and the
hijacker of the oxygen of publicity
on which they depend.

Margaret Thatcher

All attempts to destroy democracy
by terrorism will fail. It must be
business as usual.

Margaret Thatcher

It was sheer professionalism
and inspiration and the fact that you
really cannot have people marching
into other people's territory and
staying there.

Margaret Thatcher to The New Yorker *when asked about
the Falklands Operation*

When you stop a dictator there are
always risks, but there are great risks
in not stopping a dictator.

Margaret Thatcher

If they are invaded,
we have got to
get them back.

Margaret Thatcher on the Falklands

A world without nuclear weapons
would be less stable and more
dangerous for all of us.

Margaret Thatcher

The Russians put guns before butter.
We put just about everything
before guns.

Margaret Thatcher

There is no need for Europeans to quake before any threat from the Soviet colossus.

Margaret Thatcher

Soviet military power will not disappear just because we refuse to look at it.

Margaret Thatcher

Perhaps some people in the Labour Party think we are on the same side as the Russians!

Margaret Thatcher

… a gentleman on the staff of *Pravda* accused me of trying on Churchill's trousers.

Margaret Thatcher on ensuring peace with the Atlantic Alliance

Following England's loss to
Germany in the 1990 football
World Cup semi-final:
Kenneth Clarke: Isn't it terrible about
losing to the Germans at our national
sport, Prime Minister?
Margaret Thatcher: I shouldn't worry
too much – we've beaten them twice
this century at theirs.

The supreme task of
modern statesmanship is the
prevention of war.

Margaret Thatcher

Prime Minister, you are
talking too much.

*A note from Lord Carrington to Margaret Thatcher during a
meeting with the Chinese Prime Minister*

TAKING IT
ON THE CHIN

If my critics saw me walking over the Thames they would say it was because I couldn't swim.

Margaret Thatcher

I always cheer up immensely if an attack is particularly wounding because I think, well, if they attack one personally, it means they have not a single political argument left.

Margaret Thatcher

When hecklers stand up, I get a
mental jump for joy. It gives me
something to get my teeth into –
and the audiences love it.

Margaret Thatcher

I don't expect anyone just to sit there
and agree with me, that's not their job.

Margaret Thatcher

We were told our campaign
wasn't sufficiently slick. We regard
that as a compliment.

Margaret Thatcher

The Honourable Gentleman should
cast the mote out of his own eye
before he starts criticising us.

*Margaret Thatcher to Labour MP Bob Cryer on his criticism
of her dealings with the TUC, 14 June 1978*

I do love an argument.

Margaret Thatcher

If you just set out to be liked, you would be prepared to compromise on anything at any time, and you would achieve nothing.

Margaret Thatcher

I don't mind taking stick.

Margaret Thatcher

LAYING DOWN
THE LAW

To govern is to choose. To appear
to be unable to choose is to appear
to be unable to govern.

Nigel Lawson

We already have a sabbatical system.
It's called opposition, and I've had
enough of it.

Nigel Lawson

There has always been, and there always will be, an economic cycle.

Nigel Lawson

Shut up, Prime Minister.

Nigel Lawson

I'm making some changes,
Geoffrey, and they will involve
the Foreign Office.

Margaret Thatcher telling Howe of his sacking

Has he resigned or has he
gone for a pee?

Margaret Thatcher on Michael Heseltine's resignation

I wouldn't treat my gamekeeper the
way that woman treated me.

*Lord Christopher Soames on Margaret Thatcher and his
sacking from the cabinet in 1981*

I was a
reluctant butcher.

*Margaret Thatcher on
re-shuffling the Cabinet*

We in the Conservative Party
believe that Britain is still great.

Margaret Thatcher

Unless we change our ways... our
greatness as a nation will soon be a
footnote in the history.

Margaret Thatcher

We are a British nation with
British characteristics.

Margaret Thatcher

What is right for the family
is right for Britain.

Margaret Thatcher

This country belongs to the
courageous, not the timid.

Margaret Thatcher

Britain turned her face to
the world and prospered.

Margaret Thatcher

Is the nation ready to face reality?
I believe that it is.

Margaret Thatcher

The world bought British
and British was best.

Margaret Thatcher

We in Britain cannot opt
out of the world.

Margaret Thatcher

Once again, Britain stands
tall in the councils of Europe
and of the world.

Margaret Thatcher

Great Britain
is great again.

Margaret Thatcher

For to be Conservatives means
that we put our country
first in all things.

Margaret Thatcher

We know that Britain has been
in dire straits before, and that
she has recovered.

Margaret Thatcher

EUROPE

I have very strong views about Europe.
We're quite the best country.

Margaret Thatcher

I think it is very silly to get on a train
if you do not know its destination,
very silly indeed.

Margaret Thatcher

We will not tolerate Britain becoming
the poor relation of Europe.

Margaret Thatcher

Europe is a monument to the vanity
of individuals, a programme whose
inevitable destiny is failure.

Margaret Thatcher

We are no
longer the sick
man of Europe.

Margaret Thatcher

Certainly we want to see Europe more
united and with a greater sense of
common purpose.

Margaret Thatcher

Europe will be stronger precisely
because it has France as France, Spain
as Spain and Britain as Britain.

Margaret Thatcher

We believe in a free Europe but not a
standardised Europe.

Margaret Thatcher

We long for the freer movement of
people and ideas.

Margaret Thatcher

The intellectual and material richness
of Europe lies in its variety.

Margaret Thatcher

Europe is a product of history.
America is a product of philosophy.

Margaret Thatcher

Only if we speak together
can we expect the world to
heed the voice of Europe.

Margaret Thatcher

We British are as much heirs to the legacy of European culture as any other nation.

Margaret Thatcher

… we British have in a very special way contributed to Europe.

Margaret Thatcher

We can't go on any longer being Europe's most bountiful benefactor.

Margaret Thatcher

Mr Chairman, you have invited
me to speak on the subject of Britain
and Europe. Perhaps I should
congratulate you on your courage.
If you believe some of the things
said and written about my views on
Europe, it must seem rather
like inviting Genghis Khan to speak
on the virtues of peaceful coexistence!

Margaret Thatcher during a speech to the College of Europe,
20 September 1988

DEAR JOHN...

The politician who never made a
mistake never made a decision.

John Major

The first requirement of politics is
not intellect or stamina, but patience.
Politics is a very long run game and the
tortoise will usually beat the hare.

John Major

I am walking over hot coals suspended
over a deep pit at the bottom of
which are a large number of vipers
baring their fangs.

John Major

A consensus politician is someone who
does something that he doesn't believe
is right because it keeps people quiet
when he does it.

John Major

Society needs to condemn a little more
and understand a little less.

John Major

If the answer is more politicians, you
are asking the wrong question.

John Major

A sound bite never buttered
any parsnips.

John Major

A country of long shadows on county
cricket grounds, warm beer, green
suburbs, dog lovers, and old maids
cycling to holy communion through
the morning mist.

John Major on Great Britain

Nothing makes me more determined
to do something than someone
telling me I can't.

John Major

Only in Britain could it be thought
a defect to be too clever by half. The
probability is that too many people
are too stupid by three-quarters.

John Major

I am not running as Son of Margaret
Thatcher. I have my own priorities
and my own programmes.

John Major

Some people eat eggs, I wear them.

*John Major, after an egg has splattered his suit during the
1992 election campaign*

MONEY MAKES
THE WORLD
GO ROUND

The secret of happiness is to live within your income and pay your bills on time.

Margaret Thatcher

No one would remember the Good Samaritan if he had only had good intentions. He had money as well.

Margaret Thatcher

Pennies don't fall from heaven, they have to be earned here on earth.

Margaret Thatcher

It is not the creation of wealth that is wrong, but the love of money for its own sake.

Margaret Thatcher

The evil of inflation is still with us.

Margaret Thatcher

Everything a politician promises…
has to be paid for either by higher
taxation or by borrowing.

Margaret Thatcher

I do wish I had brought my cheque
book. I don't believe in credit cards.

*Margaret Thatcher at the Ideal Home Exhibition
in March 1990*

There are too
few rich and
too few profits.

Margaret Thatcher

If you go into what I call a bubble
boom, every bubble bursts.

Margaret Thatcher

Economics are the method;
the object is to change the soul.

Margaret Thatcher

You and I come by road or rail, but
economists travel on infrastructure.

Margaret Thatcher

I am always proud when Conservative
councils are economical in their use
of other people's money.

Margaret Thatcher

The Government have no money on their
own. There is only taxpayer's money.

Margaret Thatcher

The world is wracked by economic
confusion and inflation.

Margaret Thatcher

Some of you will say that taxation
is like shearing sheep – you ought
to stop when you get to the skin.

Margaret Thatcher in a speech to Tory Trade Unionists,
November 1979

I must be frank, interest rates could
be lower if governments weren't the
last of the big spenders.

Margaret Thatcher

A nation can't go on living
beyond its means.

Margaret Thatcher

Wealth must be created before
it can be shared and enjoyed.

Margaret Thatcher

There is no crock of gold
that we can raid.

Margaret Thatcher

THERE'S NO SUCH THING AS SOCIETY

We want a society where people
are free to make choices, to make
mistakes, to be generous and
compassionate.

Margaret Thatcher

I want everyone to be a man
of property; that's the way
we'll get one nation.

Margaret Thatcher

The family is the basic unit of our society. It is within the family that the next generation is nurtured.

Margaret Thatcher

I think we've been through a period where too many people have been given to understand that if they have a problem, it's the government's job to cope with it.

Margaret Thatcher

They are casting their problems
at society. And, you know, there's
no such thing as society.

Margaret Thatcher

Let us resolve to heal the wounds
of a divided nation.

Margaret Thatcher

I don't know exactly what democracy
is. But we need more of it.

Margaret Thatcher

It is the people's turn to speak.
It is their powers of which we
are the custodians.

Margaret Thatcher

Our choice will determine the life or
death of our kind of society.

Margaret Thatcher

Tradition affects a nation no less than individuals.

Margaret Thatcher

What is opportunity if your only
opportunity is to be equal?

Margaret Thatcher

To cure the British disease with
socialism was like trying to cure
leukaemia with leeches.

Margaret Thatcher

FIGHTING WORDS

The desire to win is born in
most of us. The will to win is
a matter of training. The manner
of winning is a matter of honour.

Margaret Thatcher

If you want to cut your own throat,
don't come to me for a bandage.

Margaret Thatcher

Failure?
The possibilities do not exist.

Margaret Thatcher

After being defeated by Michael
Heseltine for Tory leadership,
November 1990:
I fight on, I fight to win.

Margaret Thatcher

The fight-back
begins now!

Margaret Thatcher

The Government wants a peaceful settlement. But we totally reject a peaceful sell-out.

Margaret Thatcher

It is exciting to have a real crisis on your hands, when you have spent half your political life dealing with humdrum issues like the environment.

Margaret Thatcher

If someone is confronting our essential
liberties, if someone is inflicting injuries
and harm, by God I'll confront them!

Margaret Thatcher

It's no good dreaming about U-turns.
There are none available.

Margaret Thatcher

I said at the start I shall get things
right in the end, and I shall.

Margaret Thatcher

When I'm out of politics I'm going
to run a business, it'll be called
'Rent-a-Spine'.

Margaret Thatcher

A QUESTION
OF CLASS

After all, aren't I working class?
I work jolly hard, I can tell you.

Margaret Thatcher

I hate class. It seems to stem from the
early days of class, clash, conflict.

Margaret Thatcher

I'm not as posh as I sound. I'm not
grand at all.

Margaret Thatcher

Let our children grow tall, and some taller than others if they have it in them to do so.

Margaret Thatcher

Things that I learned… in a very modest home, are just the things that I believe have won the election.

Margaret Thatcher

The charm of Britain has always been the ease with which one can move into the middle class.

Margaret Thatcher

I want to get totally rid of class distinction. As someone put it in one of the papers this morning: Marks and Spencer have triumphed over Karl Marx and Engels.

Margaret Thatcher

YOU HEARD IT
FROM HURD

Some people find it difficult to argue
with a woman prime minister
and shrivel up.

Douglas Hurd

People are very interested in politics,
they just don't like it labelled politics.

Douglas Hurd

History provides no precise guidelines.

Douglas Hurd

Wisely used history can give pleasure
and provide us with a useful tool; but
we should not become its slaves.

Douglas Hurd

We must admit that history is
enjoyable to a large extent because
it enables us to pass judgement
on the past.

Douglas Hurd

We should be wary of politicians who profess to follow history while only noticing those signposts of history that point in the direction which they themselves already favour.

Douglas Hurd

Silence is regarded as a sort of sin now, and it has to be filled with a lot of gossip and sound bites.

Douglas Hurd, 2001

A GLITTERING
CAREER

I suppose I was about twenty…
Suddenly it was crystallised for me.
I knew.

Margaret Thatcher on going into politics

I don't want to give my life over
entirely to politics. I don't think I'd
have the ability and I'd never be
given the chance.

Margaret Thatcher in an interview with The Sunday Times,
5 March 1967

I am very pleased
with my promotion
to prime minister.

Margaret Thatcher

There is much to do and I hope
you will allow me time to do it
thoughtfully and well.

Margaret Thatcher

I am, as you may know, the first...
research chemist to hold this
great position.

Margaret Thatcher

To me it's like a dream that the next name in the line Harold Macmillan, Alec Douglas-Home and Edward Heath, is Margaret Thatcher. Each has brought his own style of leadership and stamp of greatness to the task. I shall take on the work with humility and dedication.

Margaret Thatcher during a press conference after winning Conservative leadership

Her Majesty The Queen has asked
me to form a new administration and
I have accepted.

Margaret Thatcher

I hope that where I have led, others
may follow – but not too soon.

Margaret Thatcher

The job you have given me is at once a supreme honour and the greatest possible challenge.

Margaret Thatcher

The country might in some ways be a chillier, bumpier, less cosy place – but infinitely more invigorating.

Margaret Thatcher during her second term in office, February 1984

I promise you this – I won't make
empty promises.

Margaret Thatcher

I much prefer this job to the other.

Margaret Thatcher

Winning an election is
a splendid thing.

Margaret Thatcher

LIFE LESSONS

Don't envy the success of others –
applaud it.

Margaret Thatcher

Yesterday's exaggeration is today's
understatement.

Margaret Thatcher

Above all, never throw in the towel
when you are within an ace of success.

Margaret Thatcher

I do not think it advisable to seek
head-on clashes on great issues.

Margaret Thatcher

Life does change, that is what makes it
different from death.

Margaret Thatcher

The more positive you become the
more enemies you make.

Margaret Thatcher

Always read. It is someone else's
concentrated experiences they have
put down on paper.

Margaret Thatcher

If you just set out to be liked... you
would achieve nothing.

Margaret Thatcher

Certain good things always
emerge out of bad things.

Margaret Thatcher

You often receive conflicting advice.
That's why it is so vital to get
your own ideas sorted out and
the reasons for them.

Margaret Thatcher

Utopia never comes, because we know
we should not like it if it did.

Margaret Thatcher

However far we may want to go,
the truth is that we can only get
there one step at a time.

Margaret Thatcher

We are sustained by the knowledge
that we ride on the crest of a
philosophical tide.

Margaret Thatcher

It is those with
conviction who
carry the day.

Margaret Thatcher

Our… parents brought us up
without trendy theories and
didn't make a bad job of it.

Margaret Thatcher

I think the cane has a place in the
training of children.

Margaret Thatcher

There are moments in our
history when we have to make
a fundamental choice.

Margaret Thatcher

CLASSIC LINES

People think that at the top there isn't much room…. My message is that there is tons of room at the top.

Margaret Thatcher

Why do you climb philosophical hills? Because they are worth climbing.

Margaret Thatcher

Things will get worse before they
get better. We did not promise
you instant sunshine.

Margaret Thatcher

Of course it's the same old story.
Truth usually is the same old story.

Margaret Thatcher

The moment the minority threatens
to become a big one, people
get frightened.

Margaret Thatcher

So much has been promised in the
past, so much has come to nothing.

Margaret Thatcher

Where law ends,
tyranny begins.

Margaret Thatcher

To claim a social conscience in
these circumstances can fairly
be described as humbug.

Margaret Thatcher

This is the day I
wasn't meant to see.

Margaret Thatcher on surviving an assassination plot

ON YER BIKE!

I shall present this code to Parliament like a head waiter obliged to pour a glass of Coca-Cola.

Norman Tebbit

Run a country? They couldn't run a Women's Institute raffle.

Norman Tebbit on the Labour Party

I've never bashed a union in my life.

Norman Tebbit

It's good to remember the unburied
dead and the uncollected rubbish.
Most of it can now be seen on
the Labour benches in the
House of Commons.

Norman Tebbit

Parliament must not be told a direct
untruth, but it's quite possible to allow
them to mislead themselves.

Norman Tebbit

The Conservatives played like England cricketers – too many rash strokes and run-outs, dropped catches and bowling anywhere but the stumps.

Norman Tebbit

Opinion polls are not worth the paper they are written on, in my view, through the conference season. They don't settle down again until November.

Norman Tebbit

RIGHT
HONOURABLE
FRIENDS

When the Right Honourable
Gentleman stops his troops from
fighting it.

*Margaret Thatcher, when asked when she intended to stop
fighting the last election*

May I assure the Honourable
Gentleman that my pithy comments
do not change whether I make them
at home or abroad.

Margaret Thatcher

The Honourable Gentleman is saying that he would rather that the poor were poorer, provided that the rich were less rich. That way one will never create the wealth for better social services, as we have. What a policy. Yes, he would rather have the poor poorer, provided that the rich were less rich. That is the Liberal policy.

Margaret Thatcher speaking to Liberal MP Simon Hughes

If the Honourable Gentleman will just listen, he might hear something that he did not know.

Margaret Thatcher

I am not quite certain what my Right Honourable Friend said, but we both hold precisely the same view.

Margaret Thatcher

FELLOW
POLITICIANS

Every prime minister
needs a Willie.

Margaret Thatcher on William Whitelaw

He supported me steadfastly when
I was right, and, more important,
when I wasn't.

Margaret Thatcher on William Whitelaw

He was never popular with the general public who saw what appeared to be a chain-smoking, dishevelled, languid aristocrat; by contrast, he was the object of universal respect and great affection from those who worked with him, above all his officials.

Margaret Thatcher on Nicholas Ridley

The trouble with you, John,
is that your spine does not
reach your brain.

*Margaret Thatcher on Conservative backbencher
John Whittingdale*

I simply do not understand how Ken
Clarke could lead today's Conservative
Party to anything other than disaster.

Margaret Thatcher

I would not mind betting that if Mr Gladstone were alive today he would apply to join the Conservative Party.

Margaret Thatcher

Of course they are behind me. If they were in front of me they would be the leaders.

Margaret Thatcher

John Gummer just did not have the political clout or credibility to rally the troops. I had appointed him as a sort of nightwatchman, but he seemed to have to sleep on the job.

Margaret Thatcher

Freedom will be our battle cry
and the individual will be
our watchword.

Margaret Thatcher

As long as we remain true to
ourselves we shall be a force
for freedom.

Margaret Thatcher

Let us ensure that the voice
of freedom speaks with firmness
and courage and imagination
to a troubled world.

Margaret Thatcher

Let's ensure that our children will
have cause to rejoice that we did
not forsake their freedom.

Margaret Thatcher

The actions of Government have to sustain and foster the new mood of greater freedom.

Margaret Thatcher

The ordinary people of this country also have rights against powerful institutions.

Margaret Thatcher

… we stress now the overriding need to preserve and defend the ideal and the reality of freedom.

Margaret Thatcher

We in Europe have unrivalled freedom. But we must never take it for granted.

Margaret Thatcher

There can be no
liberty unless there
is economic liberty.

Margaret Thatcher

Indeed only a truly free society
can create the resources adequate
to care for those in need.

Margaret Thatcher

We accept that democracy means
acceptance of personal responsibility.

Margaret Thatcher

The best way I know of to win
an argument is to start by being
in the right.

Lord Hailsham

A reasonable doubt is nothing
more than a doubt for which reasons
can be given. The fact that one or two
men out of 12 differ from the others
does not establish that their
doubts are reasonable.

Lord Hailsham

A great party is not to be brought
down because of a squalid affair
between a woman of easy virtue
and a proven liar.

Lord Hailsham on the Profumo scandal

Law is, of course, in a sense, no more
than a gigantic confidence trick. If
enough people did not obey the law
it would be totally unenforceable.

Lord Hailsham

The moment politics becomes dull, democracy is in danger.

Lord Hailsham

I do not believe that law can exist without sanctions.

Lord Hailsham

If the British public fall for this I will say it will be stark staring bonkers.

Lord Hailsham, on Labour's policies

DOING WHAT
YOU KNOW
IS RIGHT

Where there is discord, may we bring harmony. Where there is error, may we bring truth.

Margaret Thatcher

There is such a thing as faith that moves mountains. I have that faith.

Margaret Thatcher

Where there is doubt, may we bring faith. And where there is despair, may we bring hope.

Margaret Thatcher

To wear your heart on your sleeve isn't a very good plan; you should wear it inside, where it functions best.

Margaret Thatcher

Disciplining yourself to do what you know is right... although difficult, is the highroad to... self-esteem.

Margaret Thatcher

Ought we not to ask the media to agree among themselves a voluntary code of conduct?

Margaret Thatcher

I am in politics because of the conflict
between good and evil, and I believe
that in the end good will triumph.

Margaret Thatcher

Whatever has to be done, you
somehow find the energy to do.

Margaret Thatcher

Governments have
a duty to show
the way ahead.

Margaret Thatcher

THE END
OF AN ERA

I think I have become a bit of an institution... the sort of thing people expect to see around the place.

Margaret Thatcher

Margaret Thatcher was beyond argument a great prime minister. Her tragedy is that she may be remembered less for the brilliance of her many achievements than for the recklessness with which she later sought to impose her own increasingly uncompromising views.

Geoffrey Howe

She was at all times a politician and I was never entirely sure how much the saloon-bar xenophobia of her later years represented her own uninhibited feelings and how far she saw it as a potential vote winner.

Nigel Lawson

Normal humdrum government has been resumed.

Nicholas Ridley on the fall of Margaret Thatcher

Now it's time for a new chapter to open and I wish John Major all the luck in the world. He'll be splendidly served and he has the makings of a great prime minister, which I'm sure he'll be in very short time. Thank you very much. Goodbye.

Margaret Thatcher, 28 November 1990, remarks departing Downing Street

The world will little note nor long remember what we say, but it will not forget what we do.

Margaret Thatcher

I might have preferred iron –
but bronze will do...
It won't rust.

Margaret Thatcher on seeing for the first time the statue of
herself that was erected in the Houses of Parliament in 2007